THE ELEPHANT'S CHIROPRACTOR

Poems
by
David J. Rothman

T0159623

CONUNDRUM

cp

PRESS

Crested Butte, Colorado

ACKNOWLEDGMENTS

Some of the poems in this manuscript (occasionally in earlier versions) have appeared in the following journals to whose editors grateful acknowledgement is made:

Cafe Solo: "The Fact"

The Crab Creek Review: "Meditation and Movement at Les Terres Neuves, La Gaude"

The Crested Butte Mountain Sun: "Their Bodies and Their Voices"

The Gallatin Review: "I Think of You"

The Gettysburg Review: "You Have Caught the Screaming Baby"

The Green Mountains Review: "In Urumqi," "It Is Spring, Hangzhou," "A Stone In My Rice"

The Harvard Advocate: "Tone Rows"

The Journal: "A Life"

The Kenyon Review: "How to Eat"

The Literary Review: "The Elephant's Chiropractor," "The Septic Tank" (reprinted from Lost Creek Letters)

Lost Creek Letters: "The Septic Tank"

Manhattan Poetry Review: "Postepithalamium"

Orphic Lute: "To Be Awake," "The Solecism," "It Is Spring," "Chagall, You Are Dead"

The Pennsylvania Review: "The Apotheosis of the Saxophonist"

Poet Lore: "Disappearing Barn"

Poetry Northwest: "A Scent of Lilacs"

Quarterly West: "There is a Door"

Tar River Poetry: "The Prayers of Theodore Parker," "Four Ponies"

ISBN 0-9657159-0-6

50750

9 780965 715904

For Jacob.

CONTENTS

Prologue: A Woman Dances   1

I: A RAINBOW

Disappearing Barn   5

There is a Door   6

The Fact   7

I Think of You   8

Their Bodies and Their Voices   9

To Be Awake   10

A Rainbow   11

Return   13

II: A STONE IN MY RICE

A Stone in My Rice   17

After the Revolution   18

At the Market, Hangzhou   19

To a Rooster.   20

Old Chinese Chi Master Dances Barefoot in Broken Glass to Disco While Crowd Jeers   21

It Is Spring, Hangzhou   22

In Urumqi   23

III: THE ELEPHANT'S CHIROPRACTOR

Tone Rows   27

The Prayers of Theodore Parker   28

My Life with Matisse   29

The Apotheosis of the Saxophonist   30

Let Everyone Know You're Moving Ahead of Time   31

The Solecism   32

The Elephant's Chiropractor   33

You Have Caught the Screaming Baby   34

The Sky Does Not Compromise   35

Chagall, You Are Dead   36

The Infinite Work of Daybreak   37

IV: HOW TO EAT

Stumble   41

How to Eat   42

Meditation and Movement at Les Terres Neuves, La Gaude   43

A Scent of Lilacs   44

Small Fountain   45

Four Ponies   47

It is Spring   48

Postepithalamium   49

Good Enough   50

Going like Hello   52

The True Hydrography   53

The Lark at Fifty   55

V: GINA

Gina   59

Astoria Boulevard   61

The Septic Tank   63

A WOMAN DANCES

In my old dream, life was an awful place,
A loneliness. I thrashed and turned my face

To granite mountains or the rich sea swell,
My own reflection in the deepest well,

And you, yet none of it did any good—
It was a temporary neighborhood,

Taxed harshly by a most efficient state,
In which what was was the required rate.

In my new dream, I stand still in a field,
Enjoined to learn whatever makes it yield.

Fog and flower, toad and worm, tall grass
And I, concurrently have come to pass.

A woman dances toward me on the earth,
Holding a book that annotates each birth,

Mine, hers, yours, its, in consonants and vowels.
Sweet milk runs from her breasts. She paces, growls,

A living wave of world. Animals sigh,
Bark, sing, and whisper nothing at the sky.

A breeze suggests this time cannot last long.
And yet, upon that breeze, I hear the song

The green day chants in its own seed: I came
From nowhere, yet I am:
                                    Give me my name.

I: A RAINBOW

DISAPPEARING BARN

— for G. B.

The barn leaned toward the road,
The road curved past the barn.

The barn propped its geometry against the sky,
The sky draped the barn with stars.

Clipped cornrows questioned the barn,
The barn punctuated the fields.

A ring sanctified the moon,
The moon admired her ring.

The river breathed,
Fog ambled up from the river.

The fog slid along the ground,
The ground hid from the fog.

Fog washed over the hills,
Hills filled the fog's body.

The fog kissed the barn roof,
The barn roof flapped off like an owl.

The fog ran its hands along the barn wall slats,
One by one the slats said their goodbyes.

The car hood whispered as it cooled,
While a whisper ran its loving hand

Through the single roadside maple's leaves.
The maple's roots reached through blind dirt

And raised the evening's shoulder slightly,
The way our fingers laced

As we kissed and held each other close
Beside the disappearing barn.

THERE IS A DOOR

— for E. D. G.

There is a door that she can open now.
On one side are the quiet rooms, prepared
And bright, the windows raised, the space aired
Out, white curtains billowing inward to show
The sea's long breeze. Outside, the grasses bow
Before the prospect of a future shared:
The promise of more days like this. She's pared
Her life to this simplicity. Below,
Their friends wait for the vow each soon will say
To come down from the sky. That vow will follow
Their life until it ends and then go on,
Across the cove and out into the bay,
Arcing around its forked tail like a swallow,
A migratory bird of hope, alone.

THE FACT

— for A. Y.

1.

This is a story
No one can stand:
The fact of ending.
It flows into you
Like a draught of sand
And you cannot figure
How to make it whole.
So you accept
That the fact of a seed
And the earth issues
In a knot that unravels
Only to death.
Death, not a metaphor,
Is the master of touch —
Nature is emptiness.
So lie in the bed
And hold her close
In sleep's exhaustion.

2.

There is a story
No one can understand:
The creation of fact.
It sings out of you
Like a blossom on the sand,
And you cannot figure
How you made it whole.
Will you accept
That the fact of a seed
And the earth issues
In a knot that unravels
Death? Death,
Only a metaphor,
Is the touch of touch —
Love can fill any emptiness.
So be comforted
And hold him close
In sleep's inspiration.

I THINK OF YOU

— for J. M.

> I lie in bed and close my eyes.
> I think of you.
> I see my failure and hear my lies —
>
> But I was too young, my wise self sighs,
> To know what to do.
> I lie in bed and close my eyes
>
> But my voice becomes yours, then dies
> In my ear — you knew.
> I see my failure and hear my lies
>
> Again on the phone, your surprise
> That the only one there would be you.
> I lie in bed and close my eyes
>
> And then see you alone, affection's ties
> Cut into and then through.
> I see my failure and hear my lies
>
> About sharing that sweet accident's prize.
> But I was scared. But you were too.
> I lie in bed and close my eyes.
> I see my failure and hear my lies.

THEIR BODIES AND THEIR VOICES

— for S. T.

In the hot apartment, after dark,
The lovers will quietly sit and smoke
The day's last cigarette. They will mark
The time so many others have marked,
The complaining traffic that soon dies down
And the messy kitchen that stays a mess.
He says he'd like to go to the park
But it's late and the park is far away.
The air stands hot and thick. The town,
Alive but anonymous, like talk
Or so much of what passes for talk —
The strangely satisfying distance
Of other lights, their own resistance
To sadness after sex, an almost
Empty bottle of wine, and the gestures
Of an abandoned game of cards —
Tonight this will have to be enough.
No insight will reveal itself.
No insight will dispel the ritual
Of talk, then silence, then a book, then sleep,
The vague wish to be able to comfort each other
Possessing only bodies and voices,
Such clumsy tools. It is difficult.
And when they stumble again and again
At a thing so quiet but so important,
It makes everything else seem like a joke
On understanding and on work.

Love is a valley cultivated by exiles.
To return we must agree to labor. It is difficult.
The lovers sit and smoke in their apartment,
The windows opened out onto the dark.
A sweet breeze wanders through
As if in search of something.

TO BE AWAKE

— for A. Y.

To be awake you have to be awake
To last night's ashtray, the vision of a shoe,
And the recovered trail of one mistake
After another. Explanation falters —
For even words, although they have no bodies,
Wake up and carefully observe it's raining
And raining and raining and the mourning doves
Perch motionless, blinking, on the dark branches.
Where should they go? What should they do?
Wherever they turn they find what they already knew.
And to be awake you must be even more awake
Than those words. The drops are dripping from the gutter
In the same old way, like lovers
Who commit foolishness upon themselves
And to each other over and over,
Training words to go again and again
And again against the grain of love.

But to love you have to learn
To go again and again awake along the grain
Of love, even if you awaken in dim light and rain.
For how can you be in love for more than a minute
Without recognizing you are in love again?
Then you can awaken somewhat more,
And slip an arm over the hip and around the belly
That have come back mysteriously
To draw, murmuring, warm, together,
The way one word can draw close to another
As if carelessly, through the air.

A RAINBOW

— for E. D. G.

When I was a child, a child's eyeful,
Ordinary men and women rose into songs.
My fingers puzzled at the piano.

Then, as a corollary to perfection,
I discovered other men and women
Who grew thin roots in air — my ancestors,
Who were to be excluded from the earth.
Contempt is the favored emotion of humans,
Especially in winter, when life appears
To agree with banal arguments against itself.

So it is I learned that ordinary men and women
Are capable of extraordinary things.
How easy it is to use a gun, now and forever,
Both before and after lunch.

But now I admire the evening shower
That does not purify, but soothes us
A little, carrying the day's dirt
Away from our flesh in the flush of abundance,
Our soaped hands awkwardly following it
As formless ephemera crown us, then clothes
The ineffectual tuft and stubble of our armpits,
Endlessly resets clouded-ruby nipples,
Names bellyroll and odd back, various scars,
Imperfect geometry of genitals, buttock, thigh,
Hairy calf, journey foot, callous, and tiny toenail.
They all can will the return to each other's fingers,
The interlacing to be discovered there.
Yes. We will hold on to these bits of mud,
Of every cranky corner in, out, and around
Where water finds itself and drains,
Then returns tonight without the threat of flood,
And the afterwards when, as we dry each other off,
A song hauls full, glistening nets
From sleep's deep swell and roll
Out into the spiral of air that is our breath
So close and warm before a kiss.

If history can understand us she will see
These are the living parts calling out to the dove
As she returns like a grain of salt from the sky,
Having touched that lonely rock, Ararat,
To flutter over our heads, glorious, free,
Holding a green olive branch firmly in her beak.

RETURN

— for M. H.

The Pacific, queen of fractions,
Gazes at the constellations,
Waiting to multiply more intimate light.
A window on a ship opens.
A woman has been fighting insomnia there,
But now she turns away from that dull work.
Light filters out, breaks up on the waves
Like a hopeless attempt at seeing things
The way they are, the way they were —
It hardly seems to matter to her now.
Dissolving into nameless directions
Something in her loosens like a cry.
She wants to walk, she wants to breathe again,
So she stops studying the backlog of care
And wanders out on deck. Wind blows black foam
Back against the bow, in air so cool
And sweet she must abandon the jacket.
Because no place exists outside this salt,
She drops it overboard forever,
Another uncatalogued gift.
It vanishes like a wilting flower.
We can imagine its slow descent,
The curiosity of sharks.
Still, she's warm, she feels encumbered,
So slowly strips, piece by piece, and throws
Her clothes away until finally she herself
Is all that is left, so frail, so light,
Leaning against the rail that has slumbered
Through crossing after crossing like a fool,
But now, it seems to her, is ready to accept
That it is brass, only brass, cool, perfect brass.
She could balance on it, jump, and be enfolded.
But tonight the storms are moving into tempered climates,
And even the rocks are becoming more thoughtful,
Meditating on their own nakedness
And how they have survived it.
In her mind she might be in a field, alone,
But she is with others who gently sleep in their berths —
Lovers like pairs of hands after applause,
Everyone else like sign language.
Each dark breath she tastes is better

Than any reproach and returns
To the next dark breath
And then another and another quiet hour,
As she finally turns from the stars
And walks alone, unnoticed, sweet, and naked,
Singing only to herself,
Back to her single, living bed.

In the dawn, tropical islands glide by
Like half-forgotten kisses,
And the ship goes on unravelling the ocean
With its imperturbable propeller.

II: A STONE IN MY RICE

A STONE IN MY RICE

There was a stone that I did not see
In my rice, as I lifted it to my laughing mouth
In the heart of a sticky clump.
It must have escaped the sifting
And then steamed into its soft shell
Like a pearl's ugly heart,
Drawing the small grains around
To disguise its unhappiness. It rolled
Across my tongue like wasted time
Or a terrible, secret truth,
Until probability tossed it between my teeth,
Where it now has taken a revenge
Both silent and invisible to everyone else,
And incomprehensible
To me.

AFTER THE REVOLUTION

A quiet morning, the clouds much as before,
The mist on West Lake practicing.
I walked onto the cold, cracked tiles, yawned twice,
Turned the sink faucet, and the spigot blew out.
Old spigot, bad pipes, and no regrets.
Water sprayed against the other wall,
I laughed in that shower and reached for the soap,
Yelled "Husband, come here and help me!"
But the room began to spin, detaching itself
From the objects in it, which floated at first
Like dizzy ideas in a dialectic, then began to pick up speed
With a kind of frantic loyalty to their surroundings.
The wall cracked. Unfortunate. But a room
Is not eternal, and can be rebuilt with care.
Dust and fragments of paper, lipstick cartridges,
My careful, running signatures, a silk tie,
Handfuls of my long, black hair, Lu Hsun,
Cary Grant, and a stack of dance records
Jumped into the swirling air, then shivers of floorboard,
Darting nails, zippers, books, furniture,
Violins, dead babies, passports, Buddhist temples,
Kitchen utensils, my husband, wailing children,
Prayers, and ancestors swirled up into it,
Faster and faster, until in one single, great spasm,
The whole heaving mass of muck ripped
The tender ceiling to pieces, tore up, up,
Through our neighbors' place on the fifth floor,
Gathered them in, weeping, shredded the roof, then clouds,
And, leaving the city locked in struggle far below,
Carried us with a roar off into the deep, deep sky.

AT THE MARKET, HANGZHOU

At dawn, exotic optimism the mood,
I went to market, where the peasants stood
Prepared to make my dirty money good
On universal harmonies of food.

Some watched me buy my breakfast dumplings. "Wait.
They're cold," the ancient woman said, "just wait
A bit." She scraped the old, black dough away
To clear a bull's-eye on her frying tray,

Poured oil, then plumped a few new dumplings down.
Hundreds of suffocating fish bumped fin
In nearby tubs. One dumpling's edge turned brown.
Fish man stood up, walked over, flashed a grin.

"My fish. Buy some?" he asked. "Leave him alone,
He's buying dumplings from me today." "But say
He wants fish too. You want some fish today?"
"He doesn't, and who would? They're not full-grown,

And always bony." "Listen to her, she's crazy.
And see that dirty tray? Disgusting. Lazy."
"The only place I'm lazy is in your wish.
And young man, look. Those fish are sick. Sick fish,

Sick man. Ha ha!" "What sick? They're orange fish.
Like other orange fish. But better. See,
Still flapping. Cooked with ginger, what a dish."
"He wouldn't buy your fish if they were free!"

"Why not let him decide, dumpling windbag?"
"Breakfast is done, give me your bowl." "Some fish?"
"Leave him alone!" "You leave him alone!" "But he's mine!"
"You liar!...Dog!...Hyena!...Vulture!...Hag!"

TO A ROOSTER

Your cock-a-doodle-do days are over now.
No more struts and preens on dawn's thin walk,
No more rubber-red proud comb to bow
Down to scattered grain. No more. White cock,
Just bought and paid for, now thrown down in defeat,
Rattling off in a poor empire's bus,
Now you only open your sad eyes,
Resigned and weak, at stops. The world's old laws
Prove we eat you, so we have come
Twining tangles in your useless claws.
Struck on the lips, you have gone dumb.
Dinner points its hatchet blade at the block
Where you will catch it.
Now your neck lies stretched. Goodbye aubade,
Untrue lovers' loyal morning warning,
Caught between the inexorable finger and thumb
Of hunger.

OLD CHINESE CHI MASTER DANCES BAREFOOT IN BROKEN GLASS TO DISCO WHILE CROWD JEERS

We watched the daughter walk on eggs.
She didn't crack a single crown.
We cheered the brothers who bent down
The two-headed spear's shaft by placing
Its points against their leathery necks

And lunging toward each other, bracing
Themselves with the power of Chi-gong
Alone. But the show's gone on too long.
Like hail, sunflower seed shells fall
To show how modern youth is racing

Away from old-time spectacle
Into the new, unofficial likes
Of sunglasses and motorbikes.
Now the old man himself comes out
For one last shot at hushing the hall.

We've seen him break stones, with a shout,
Against his forehead, keep a smile
While steel sledgehammers smacked a pile
Of concrete blocks stacked on his chest.
But now he'll crush the growing doubt

Of his old art. This is the test.
Let's go. Do you have your bike-lock key?
The king is dancing on a sea
Of shards. So much one man can do.
Let's go, for now. We know the rest.

The dwindling audience chants Disco! Disco!

IT IS SPRING, HANGZHOU

I have worked here long enough.

Spring, auspicious
As Rip Cap American Flange,
Is arriving with its precious
Stuff. The pull ring sticks

Down below the soft lead
Seal and announces PULL OUT
To split and open the serrated
Proclamation: Sogrape Mateus —

Rip Cap US pats. 2760671 & 3
259149, foreign pats.
& pats. pend. Now free
To trade, Vinhos de Portugal, 187 ml.,

Bubbles a bit, happy in its little bottle
That rises through the slapped on label
(Depicting a mysterious manor), to the narrow throttle.
11.5% stands for alcohol,

Poised for import here on the lawn
As the new year rolls over
This People's Republic of Too Many People, gives a yawn
Like a waking tiger —

And twang, twang, goes the traditional music of spring.
This wine should be chilled
Before serving,
Says the sole agent, East Asiatic Co., LTD., Hong Kong,

So helpful to those so far from home, under blossoming cherry.
Little birds are twittering in the sky.
Here we go, won't be long now, it tastes good
Anywhere, sings one of them to me.

IN URUMQI

I like it here in Urumqi,
A place so many claim they hate.
The confused hovels, the sky
As clear as a mistake, afterwards,
Suit me. The workers hammer at stones by day
And far into the night, when dust storms blow
In from that dry plane where long ago
Now-smashed oases of craft grew,
The workers hammer at stones.
New but crumbling apartment buildings flank
The market, where a Uigur butcher takes a knife
And ends a sheep's short life.
He straddles it and holds the chin,
Then cuts the carotid in one easy pass
As if opening a letter. Blood squirts
On the stone. He nails the carcass up,
Cuts off a piece of flesh as his buddy
Starts to clean the guts, then holds it out,
To me. He smiles, beckons with the other hand,
The one still loosely holding the knife,
Toward the small restaurant's door.
Good! he says. I enter. I eat.

Later, I pay to watch a big talker stick
A snake headfirst into each nostril and pick
Them together out of his dangling jaw.
He spits some blood and smiles too.
He's done it before. It's killing him,
He knows it, and yet goes on. I'd tell him
Get out, fool, go to Beijing
And sell shishkabob! Prosperity's black market
Will kiss you. But I don't speak his dialect.

Happiness here hinges on such little things
As knowing what is safe to eat
And what should be avoided.
Fresh meat, if you see it healthy, raw,
Then cooked before your eyes, is fine.
But cold noodles from an outdoor stand,
Where angry flies and dirty hands conspired
In a pile of dough, should be avoided.
If you'd been here, in my position, alone
And hungry, you too might have chosen as I did,

As many cocksure travelers do,
To chance it with the cold noodles,
And now you too would be lying weak
With fever and dysentery in a dirty hotel room
Without the solace of companionship.

I've sold my useless ticket out. I'll buy another
When I'm better. Yes, I like this place,
It's like the little desert
That had been growing between us
Dune by argumentative dune, but bigger,
Unrolled, big enough for me
To wander around in on my own.

III: THE ELEPHANT'S CHIROPRACTOR

TONE ROWS

1.

A sound can remain in the silence
Which memory is. The slow healing
Of a cut hidden by clothing is the same.

One morning, water was splashing
From a stone pitcher onto white tiles;
That sound remained as the day passed.
Sunlight was water, the city was tiles;
Crowds were water, the city was tiles.

One morning, the sound of a dream remained.
Imagine the night. A wind from the Mediterranean
Blows across the fields of bamboo.
Lacroix has cut the stalks to different heights,
And they are singing chords
While he sits at home, reading by a single light.
Nearby, a forest of maple trees,
Destined to become woodwinds,
Waves bare branches at the sky.

2.

Just as a scar grows slowly strong,
And an anonymous song sticks in the memorym
My incurious dream remains submerged —
Even after rising silently
To the glittering, damaged surface of talk.
Night swirls in like the wind
That fitfully blows through fields of bamboo.
Lacroix has cut the stalks to different heights
And now air drags across their slotted, angled points
While he sits at home and reads by a single light.
He smokes his pipe and contemplates
The cadences meandering through his farm
Of future woodwind reed. In the morning,
Rain that will never reach the ground
Sparkles from the orange roof tiles.
The bamboos slowly grow in the Mediterranean wind,
Lowering the chords until,
Singing themselves together, they close,
Just as a scar grows slowly strong
And an anonymous song sticks in the memory.

THE PRAYERS OF THEODORE PARKER

From the days of my earliest boyhood —
When I went stumbling through long, tall grasses
And swimming in clear, sweet waters
Sometimes sweeter for being cold —
Honey has been building in me, drop by drop.

The other life within life, memory,
Is growing into a busy hive, hexagon
By hexagon, as all the small mortal things,
Exceedingly rich, cluster around
Each single budding sense and catechize it.

Nothing to the hills
That shrug off every day's embrace —
Nothing to the stand of birch
Whose gold leaves spark
In the crisp October breezes —
Nothing to the elements
That hold me up as evidence —
I recall my many, clear sources,
Now and always, as I drift downstream
To no apocalypse.

I will arrive there
Like a floating candle and burn
Down to a charred wick end in happiness
Before I too go out.

MY LIFE WITH MATISSE

Splash an arc of blue up here, and birds
Will start to bill curiously out of its laws,
Dancers sit laughing in the opportunity below.
Nearby, a wine press drips lightning,
And a priest whose face, an empty oval,
Is every face, opens his arms to me.
Nothing more than that will happen,
The nothing more than that
That is sufficient and intractable.

Off there paint more blue, the sea,
And here some hills, a house with white walls.
Here come young women; do you understand
That a face is just a few simple lines?
The fruit fresh from the tree is the same.
Flowers you will never find in a store
Can go on going forever when the eye
Respects their empty interiors,
The way they have been pressed
Like spring water from an invisible place,
Streaming over themselves until the brush
Becomes like the ink it moves, the charcoal
Like your hand holding an apple.

Life as an eye's hard work tracks shapes
That lurk under the rush things are.
The things are always there, riding in savage circles.
The shapes abandon talent and regret. The colors too.
Here are the sea, some hills, a breeze.
This is your warm hand touching them,
Drawing them forth.

THE APOTHEOSIS
OF THE SAXOPHONIST

The conductor stops
And raps the stand with his baton
But the saxophone player keeps playing
Old riffs again and again, in an ecstasy,
Above the absence of applause.
The audience finally wanders off like a cloud.
Later, the puzzled janitor yells
I gotta turn out the lights! and does so
But the saxophone player keeps playing
To an empty hall as the remaining fire
Condenses like tears on his glowing horn.

Then I wake up and know
It was a dream, only a dream of beauty,
Like an idiot swimming in the dark,
But the saxophone player keeps playing
To the neon sign which runs its private races
Outside the failure of my curtain and shade.
The hissing, clanking radiators punctuate
The standards which an unknown other tenant
Always practices too damn late at night.

I say he leans toward a window,
His eyes closed and beyond questions.
There is no furniture in his apartment,
He's not wearing any clothes, and he puffs
His cheeks in circular breathing to give thanks,
In phrases cranked from his saxophone,
To the blind landlady, snoring in her bed,
Who supplies the steamy rhythm in the dirty pipes.

LET EVERYONE KNOW
YOU'RE MOVING AHEAD OF TIME

— US Post Office Change of Address Kit

To dive at night from an iceberg's nose,
To take one strong, invisible step
Into the heart of an eternal rose,
To flip away from the past
Like a penny off God's careless thumb —
These desires haunt me like a crime.
Let everyone know:
I'm moving ahead of time.

There is a door we must unlock,
Though not with keys, cunning, blindness,
Or the amnesiac game of talk.
I know the sky is home to the hawk,
Who feeds upon all of us sparrows,
But who wants merely to return
To the church of the obvious,
Carrying an armful of broken arrows?
I used to do that when I made rhyme,
But now let everyone know:
I'm moving ahead of time.

My feet and I are journeying to a greater love
Than this paltry field of white can store,
One that burns but does not diminish.
At last, the end of commerce
And stupid conversations about weather!
Goodbye to the farcical war
Between the margin and the page.
Goodbye to the world of mime.
Write it on the wheels of my ankles,
And give my old man the news:
I have left. Dear, decaying mother,
Oh, my sad brother,
I am beyond, before, outside.
I've moved ahead of time.

THE SOLECISM

In those wonderful days I knew
I could not possibly repay my debt,
So I spent the mornings insulting work
And gave everything I owned away.
The old couch sighed once
Before crumbling into the porch.

It was then that I discovered
The mystery and melancholy of a street.
The arches of the ancient building
Whose name remains empty
Marched into the zero of perspective.
The evenings themselves meandered with me,
Exploring the deserted marketplaces.
When the vendors began, in darkness,
Carefully, professionally, dispassionately to lay out
Today's fish and meat on the knife-scored counters
We would go home, arm in arm, to drink wine.

Time, like a drunk's hand, held things clumsily.
I lived without connections, a well-turned phrase
In the private jazz that passes by
Like a rolling hoop.

It was a kind of grammar grafted onto grammar
That I began to hear, a series of infinite divisions
Corrupting the dialect of the capital
With the names of that distant province
Where artisans still throw pots on the wheel.

No rage could disturb my solitude.
No liquor could crack open the riddles.
No ordinary citizen ever knew my pity
Even if his sneakers were laced with rubber bands.
Come on friend, I finally said to one
Sing something we can dance to —
The perfection of Vitruvian courtyards,
Or the story of an angel, or the sun
Rising like a dove from its olive perch.

THE ELEPHANT'S CHIROPRACTOR

1.

It was all arranged. The press
Would be there, under the tent,
As the clowns stood awed in the sawdust,
Hands on their twisted hips.
I would stand on a scaffold,
The massive beast beneath me,
A rubber mallet in my hands, poised
Like God on the Sistine ceiling
About to deliver the gift:
A spine so huge, a spine so straight!

2.

The mallet dropped in the right
Place, and that giant lumbar kicked
Back into spot like a rifle shot,
Setting off a celebration,
A marquee of flashbulbs.
The handle rang sweetly in my hands
While the clowns applauded
And the elephant knelt in gratitude.

3.

My victories accrue:
The jawbones of whales,
The notocords of ancient mammals.
I cure tuberculariaceae,
Up to my elbows in the earth,
I reproduce entire species from a single hair,
Adjust unborn children in the womb.
Even the time, I know, is out of joint —
I walk the streets at noon,
My hands grasping, twisting air.

YOU HAVE CAUGHT
THE SCREAMING BABY

You come to a page of news.
Once it was empty,
But now words squat all over it,
Staring in surprise at you
Because you caught the screaming baby
Allegedly thrown through
A closed fourth floor window.

Out of a sparkling halo of glass
Dropped the screaming baby
Whom you caught, let us not be naive,
In an involuntary, if praiseworthy, move.
Now two heads peer over the fourth story ledge,
Shattered sunlight litters the pavement,
And a crowd crunches over it from all directions.
Two officers arrive, draw their guns,
Charge apprehensively up the stairs,
Scuffle with, cuff, and then return with a man.
Shortly after, a crying woman with a bruised cheek
Comes up to you and says Thank you
For catching my baby. It was my ex.
He's a son of a bitch.

You are the one who was there,
And now you are one of the ones who have read
The words you have become,
That stare back in surprise at you
Because you caught the screaming baby
And held her in your arms.

THE SKY DOES NOT COMPROMISE

No need to move, round, blue, eternal theater
Where travelling clouds, swallows, fire,
And the rain that looks for my upturned face
Improvise their circular script.

Unlike the first barbarian, who sat on his horse,
Cradling a spear and talking to himself
In an unintelligible dialect,
I will begin to bridge the rift between us.
After all, it is spring. The black fields
Are no longer playing dead,
Or even congratulating themselves
On the perfection of winter.
In the same way, after I die
I plan to become uncanny,
Roots curling through the hole
Where my nose once worked,
Buds pushing out of my hands.

Life will undo me, and so I turn to you.
Greetings! No need to move. I promise
That when I have departed
From the agony of the street
I will no longer be a place
Where incompatible desires meet.

I raised my arms and stood
Like a puddle on the sidewalk.

CHAGALL, YOU ARE DEAD

Chagall, you are dead
Unlike the man with a gashed forehead
Who passed me in the street, crying,
Or the eyes-closed couple kissing on the subway,
Or the painters who live in dirty corners
And stir their soup while dreaming "blue."
Alive we bite the curious seed at an apple's heart
In Paris, 1910, arriving, pregnant
With the subterranean secret of color.

Chagall, you are dead, but from the glittering gutter
Where you throw me I float, an ox's nose,
Measured, remembering, and supernatural,
Over Vitebsk. The lovers knock,
Marriage triumphs over gravity in a stroke
As they caress each other and whisper
Only love interests us, and we will touch
Only those things that revolve around love.
A violin complains, ten thousand weddings
Celebrate the opening of the bottle
Recycling center over on Sixth Avenue.

Chagall, you are dead. Yet, strangely, it is time
To pull the ram from the thicket,
Sing on the roof, spread our lives out into city haze
And the memory of a muddy street.
Courage, sweet patch of sky with angel.
Stay with me forever, I beg you,
Live with me like the color of my eyes —
No mere reflection of blue.

THE INFINITE WORK OF DAYBREAK

The infinite work of daybreak crosses the world
A line dividing light from dark and darkness.
It makes each hour and every eye embark
Into particular replies, like trees.

Still, you imagine the ocean swell by swell
In darkness, out to where the line of dawn
Trails ragged curtains through doldrum and storm
Toward this smooth lip of sand. Here small black waves
Rise, curl, then break to spreading bars of foam
Which murmur up the beach into the visible.
The waves collapse into smooth apron shallows.
And when the infinite daybreak reaches them,
Outfiguring blank depths and tidal keys,
The history of their stoic generation —
The earth and moon and sun and wind and time
All moving like a mindless algorithm —
They'll send blue streaming, blue announcing more.

Now points above the shimmering horizon
In growing dimmer signify the wing
Of love, however wild, however dark.
For there is always loving as today
Arrives, for love must cross imagined distances
To play in royal coconut palm crowns.

If you have ever stood and waited for
The infinite work of daybreak to arrive,
Be blessed in its innumerable hours,
And counting them, go out into the day.

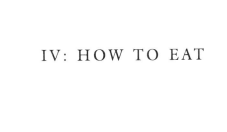

IV: HOW TO EAT

STUMBLE

— for E. B. R.

My first memory is of running towards a French door.
I was a horse and rushing down the hall
Of first times, as everyone does
Until they lurch ahead of where the body can go.

I didn't see what I have to remember now,
What could have been avoided and put off
Until a more graceful entrance to the then and there
Suggested itself. My left hand shattered one

Small pane, glass scattered across the living-room floor
As I pulled back a new arm, the torn one
That had suddenly become my own. I
Was lucky that time, I didn't wind up

As I may yet, blindly clutching the wheel
Behind the smashed windshield of some numb force
That cannot be appeased. Instead I became
One more stray bullet whistling out of the senseless world

Into the senseless world, one more fingering
On the suicide slide that will never shock
This place into remembering what we can.
Its figure is of what it makes,

Always stumbling to self-slaughter as I did,
Killing itself with inevitable mistakes.
So the memories I hold so dearly,
Like a lover's body, reveal.

They sleep on my left side,
In the snake-shaped scar, whispering
Be ready with tenderness —
No one is coming for this unlucky world

The way your mother came for you
To stop the blood with a towel, gently,
Before it was too late.

HOW TO EAT

— for L. Y.

My mother's mother's father made a table.
To build the top he shaped irregular wood
Into geometry. Each square's corners
Center the sides of the next largest square,
From heart to edge, like the genealogy
We always find ourselves making.
One Thanksgiving, surrounded by everything,
Lester, my mother's mother's brother,
The wrestler, autodidact polymath
And self-made man, discovered
Chopped liver in a blue bowl
Resting there, on his dead father's table:

    1 lb. liver fried in chicken fat
    2 large onions fried in chicken fat till transparent
    Chop with three hard boiled eggs. Add 1 tspn. salt
    More fat to taste, several chopped scallions
    If available —

A delicacy Lester, who has gout,
Knew he should not love too much.

He sat down in his niece's house
At that dead father's table
To his sister's old recipe
A copy of which, framed by brittle tape,
Survives in my mother's three-ring scraps.
He carefully scooped and spread chopped liver
On a salty cracker, ignoring his family,
The other guests, his tomato juice,
Nearby cranberry sauces, sliced turkey,
Marinated mushrooms, peanuts, salads,
Sweet squash, and crisp, new fruit
That had been patiently growing for months —
The rich stuffing of a real prosperity —
And any of the other temptations that beset appetite
With infinity and therefore failure.

He ate slowly, closing his eyes after each of two bites
Like a man who has learned the various forms of judgment
Breathing deeply in his body. His bald head shone
And he savored that small thing.

MEDITATION AND MOVEMENT
AT LES TERRES NEUVES, LA GAUDE

If you cannot accept the landscape
You must create another.
Things happen in places, there's no escape —
The womb is inside the mother.
And something real gave birth
To these hilltop villages that overlook the sea.
Does anyone living know how the earth
Was captured and rebuilt
To set its bright light free?

No. And these are just small cities
The dead built to defend,
Overrun long ago and now inconsequential.

The moon, sorrowful engine,
Is driving around St. Paul de Vence.

It should be possible
For a wall to be ordinary and yet full
Of possibility like these,
Where each crooked stone's space
Has been researched by a pair of hands.
It should be possible to believe
In making a bright and loving human place.

A man decided to throw himself away.
Someone aboard saw this last choice and yanked
The emergency brake, arresting punctuality
Like a common thief escaping through a field.
We sat and steamed impressively, all power.
There was nothing to do but read, be curious,
And talk. I met a woman. We discussed
The perfection of the shifting summer shadows
On a nearby town. We imagined sitting there,
On the piazza, escaped from this hot train,
And eating gelato in those shadows — facts,
We allowed, that could slowly crawl across a man's
Desperate and similar hunger to depart,
Then take him by the hand out to this place.
Now a line of question marks appeared in windows,
Craning their necks as if at a tennis match.
There was a scent of lilacs on the breeze
As representatives of the local powers
Arrived to take a look and scratch their heads
Before they carefully zipped the sheeted suicide
Into a cloudy plastic bag. They talked,
We tried to overhear their stories. They cracked
His dusty wallet for a history,
But found no words, only a few small men
With crumpled faces. They tried to give a name
To everything but only took it away.
The sun blared like a television sun.
It's always just like this, the sudden departure
From the ordinary back into the ordinary.
In an hour our car complained, jerked twice, lurched,
And punctuated by a metallic crunch
The train moved out while the body bounced off down
The easy road that leads to the house of the dead.
We found our places again. The conductor spoke.
He apologized to us, he thanked us quietly
For all our patience, and then, after a pause,
Announced the dining car was open for lunch.

SMALL FOUNTAIN

New water has risen here for centuries,
To find itself forced higher up in stone.
It arcs from four small smooth brass lion heads
With spigot mouths, and threads four holes in blank,
Surrounding marble slab. Precise approach
Of gravity and time in silence, the water
Is clearer and more sweet than other water,
Or so we who live near this old square believe.
So we come here to sit and meet each other,
To stroll and innovate ourselves with talk.
Now in the hot afternoon my father wets
A cloth to cool his balding head and smiles
As water runs onto his work-soiled shirt.
His cronies argue how to rule the country.
The fountain weaves like antiphonal trombones
Which echoed first off St. Marks' curving tile,
Unlocking secrets of modern harmony.

But the fountain is a truncated, ribbed column
Of cracked concrete. One dented tube juts out,
Where water falls like news from an injured angel.
An indecipherable banality
Has clogged two of the holes in the crumbling stone.
A puddle collects at the only other hole,
Where it slowly drains through burnt-out cigarettes.
A couple squabbles more and more insistently
In a second story apartment across the way,
Until the man comes out on the balcony
In undershirt, leans on the grill exasperated,
And looks at nothing in particular,
And then the fountain, while the woman yells
At him from just inside. He goes back in,
And starts to yell again. A man sees me
Examining the fountain, and curses it.
He explains its spigot broke one of his teeth
When he was young and stupid, drunk and thirsty,
And trying to suck straight from the source one night.

But all the springs that still bring water up
Go streaming to the flood. The men and women
Who live here fill their buckets, and then turn
Work into soapy brooks that gurgle off
Circuitously into the Adriatic.

I cup my hands, sip twice, and a voice says "Blink.
Yes, this is Veronese, this Carpaccio.
Yes, this is Titian's blue, the color of hope,
Rising to heaven. This is Moses striking
Your heart in the desert, through Tintoretto's eye."
And later on, such water mixes with wine,
Sparks the red lips of August's desire, and thanks
The shimmering stars for falling into the sea.

Now I am singing the dog's end of a song
And stumbling homeward arm in arm with water,
Who's drunk and claims she's happy to have lived
Just once, "Just once," she babbles, "Just once, once."
She wavers slightly as we part company
And she tumbles back into her dark pensione,
From which she will soon plash laughing back out,
Not without grace, from the real fountain again,
A rope coiling through stone, tying together
The detritus that all things must become.

FOUR PONIES

Four ponies are standing in a parking lot.
They wear brightly colored saddle blankets.
Their faded leather harnesses sparkle with bells.
They shift their feet a little. They slowly chew.
One lifts his tail and takes a grassy crap.

The ponies stand at the compass points
Of a four-armed metal wheel that turns on a child's whim.
It is hot out, there is no grass, and the ponies
Cannot leave the circle because their bridles
Knot high and close on the metal wheel.

They don't seem to mind. They do not stamp
Or shy from the fat, dirty man who owns them.
Most of the time, he sits on a rickety chair nearby,
Scratching his stubble and watching the cars.
Unlike an angel, he needs to eat.

Sometimes the ring the ponies always walk
Moves outward like watery circles from a stone.
In the end their harnesses rot through, fall off
And they run in a field together,
Ears back, bobbing their heads.

But to return: most of the time they stand in the heat
Unmoving, inarticulate. The traffic continues
Because this is a city. The ponies shrink
And vanish in the rearview mirror:
Four ponies walking circles in a parking lot.

IT IS SPRING

A red finch is singing in the chestnut tree.
The buds pout in the rain, swaying the branches.
Smoke swirls into the gray sky
From a source the rooftops hide.
The rain falls straight down,
Then slants, then stops.
A few notes, and the faces of strangers emerge
From themselves and become understandable.
Delicate dogwood rushes past.

Surprise, the willows chime in two days later,
Sprouting blond tresses and tossing their heads
In the fine-toothed wind that soon
Will run over furrows, dry sweat from backs,
And snap attention from the sheets
On lines through the city —
You have not wasted your life.

POSTEPITHALAMIUM

— for Jimmy and Helena Butler, and their daughter Devon

In the America of sunlight, fast cars,
And rock and roll, I forgot the names of women
I had scribbled hurriedly on slips of paper.
I know they forgot mine too, again and again,
Although we enjoyed sitting in bars
And talking about nothing for hours.
Our youth made the most ordinary things
Seem endlessly fascinating.

Now a historian perches
On all those quick, easy insights,
Annotating the difficulties
Of getting from one place to another.

This is how I've come to admire the beach
That seems to stretch out of sight.
There the clouds disperse, move in,
And then disperse again.

All day we lay on towels, talking, talking,
And drinking wine. In the evening Devon slept.
Breakers pitched themselves on the indifferent sand.
From where we sat, the patio whose cracked slates
Give back each day's warmth, we could hear them
The way you can hear another heart, sometimes,
Through the insistence of your own.
The forgettable conversation we made among ourselves
Dissipated in the steady seabreeze —
The fact of one more day's affectionate tug —
And afterwards we sat without talking for a while.
Then Helena said, as if it were so obvious,
What only became obvious because she said it:
That's such a comforting sound.
Really, it's the most comforting sound.

GOOD ENOUGH

— for Emile Hebert

Emile Hebert never hit his students
The way he said the great Kovar hit him
With whatever he happened to be eating
In the moment of an unmusical offering.

Kovar with chicken leg: "Are you stupid,
Or too lazy to practice? Don't waste my time!"
Kovar gets up, walks to the door, opens it.
"Go home. I thought you had talent,
But now I wonder. Are you sure you want
To be a musician? Do you want to play the bassoon?"

That's how I pictured it at fifteen,
Hearing the story from Emile, who sang off-key
And swayed in a chair, waving a pencil from another planet
As I agonized Bertoni, Piard, Milde, Bozze, Gambaro,
The opening phrase of "Rite of Spring," or the Bolero.
"The music is better than these mistakes,"
He would say, then snatch his horn from its stand
And air-brush my blindness out of a song.

Sometimes I too could taste the perfection
He drank as if from a fountain
In the overtones of doubled cane,
Where good enough is never good enough.
Sometimes I wondered if it did exist.
Then "Good enough?" Emile would roar,
"You say you think that's good enough?
OK! Good enough! This lesson is over!
Give me your ten dollars and get out! Come back
When you want to learn about music."

My scales still wander up and down
Like angels with too many thumbs.
The keys, silver jongleurs, laugh and wink
With the secrets of embouchure,
Far simpler than its technique,
Although more difficult to describe,
Like the sun, or love, which also cannot be compared
To anything else that actually exists.

But what is this laughter within me,
Rippling and gliding like chianti
Although I practice a book
That cannot lead to heaven or even praise?
On each page scribbles ripple like the impossible high E
Wagner buried in the Tannhäuser overture
Where doubled cello chaos makes it pointless anyways.
And my left index finger slips
Imprecisely across the half hole,
Breaking key notes in half.
What is this rippling laughter?

Emile, no man performs his corollaries,
Yet yours proceed from that musty room
Where I took my lessons, and greatness
Was pouring from your priceless Heckel
That had been cured for six months in banana oil
To find a rich, full sympathy with air.
These days when honey buzzes from bassoons I know
Good enough must be good enough at other times.
For example, when lovers look each other in the eye
And touch without the benefit of music,
The notes crack very easily.
And when words must measure out
Impossible sorrows, or even the joy of learning,
How can their ratio be good enough?
Surely you knew that truth, and others still beyond it,
And that is why you insisted
That in the one realm where it can be true,
Where laughter can well up from maples into daylight,
Good enough is never good enough.

GOING LIKE HELLO

— for Bill Ripley

He drove a great white shark,
Fins, pink upholstery, bad steering, the works.
So when I see those old Ambassadors,
Cadillacs, Pontiacs, loyal rockets
Rustily lumbering around corners,
I catch myself going like hello,
As if I might suddenly bark.
As if this all were a comedy
And we were still drinking our way,
Singing our way across the Utah desert
Toward perfections of irresponsibility,
Laughing at a slippery ribbon of midnight,
I go like hello to greet the car
That is not his car. Then, in a kind of tomorrow,
I watch the machine that need has marked
And remarked with errands and mistakes
Glide by, glide by, going like goodbye.

THE TRUE HYDROGRAPHY

— for N. H.

1.

What is more sad than a wedding day
Dissolving into nothing new?
The caterer calls off his crew,
The guests slink quietly away

Like crooks, and fold their flowery prints
Back onto hangers, into bags.
One already drunk uncle zags
Back home. Close friends and parents wince.

I worked at comfort, though I know
That sympathy is not enough
For such occasions. The sun can't bluff
The stars at dusk. It's time to go.

And he will go, back to his place,
Where things still work, the car, the door,
The telephone. Water will pour
With typically indifferent grace,

From cloud to ground, and easily
From cup to throat, taking each day
A bit downstream from this dismay.
This is the true hydrography.

Just as the Paris gutters swell
With streams from hidden wells despite
Whatever mayhem filled the night,
I pray for time to serve him well.

He laughs through tears, says "This is nuts,"
And "Thanks," and "Sorry." Then more tears.
Despite the finely meshing gears
Of friendship I feel like a klutz.

For the laws of water also hold
No man or woman can succeed
In shouldering another's need
For water and its manifold.

2.

Afterwards, street lamps showered
That conversation with commentary,
As I tried to explain how real unhappiness
Is a spring as deep as anything,
Always there, impossible to untell,
And something everyone has always known.
"Let's stay out all night," she said.
Why sit at home reading, brow furrowed,
Neither waiting nor not waiting,
While my lips become a ghost's?"

Neil, she was right —
What a kiss that was! like life itself,
The many kinds of sadness and of joy
Merging yet continuing, like waves.

THE LARK AT FIFTY

— for Kurt Brown

For years he woke at night, one eye on morning,
A distant, promised fact. He blindly sang
To all the men and women, young and old,
Who passed his branch, or lay to sleep beneath it
In love, or from exhaustion, or with loneliness.
Grown gray, reflexive, he has given up
His sweet dominion. Dawn: he thinks a thought
Of silence while the hills ignite with nothing.

                            How praise what isn't?
He asks, and shifts a little on his twig.
He is Alaudidae Sulking, a melancholy
And stubborn bird, a menopause with wings.
These days I like the way the bluejay sings
He says, and snickers in his shiny feathers.
You'll catch him perched and brooding, eyeing you,
Then wonder why the day is long and flat.

V: GINA

GINA

A woman is yelling the name "Elvira!"
Regularly, questioningly, loudly,
With the same inflection every time —
The first syllable weak, strong, equal force on the next two.
She leans out of a tenement window,
Looking around, down over the laundry lines,
Expecting something to happen, some response,
As if her voice were a lever.
But there is nothing, just the voice
Of a woman yelling, over and over, the name "Elvira!"
Which rides unappeased over rooftops,
And navigates streets and alleys,
A slogan looking for a revolution.

This invisible woman, hollering anonymous,
Pauses long enough to suggest silence,
Then yells again, or sometimes doesn't for a while
But soon starts up as if this were the past.
So relentless, she could be an angel
Carrying an incomprehensible message.
Celestial, she hovers over the city and sings
Like an engine, or summer, or rain,
Or a diffuse, impermeable principle
That demands attention — oblivion, or birth —
But refuses to be understood.

The woman yells the name "Elvira!"
And she has now been chanting the name "Elvira!"
On and off for half an hour, always the same,
Until I too have begun to whisper the name "Elvira!"
As I sit watching the traffic, "Elvira!"
As I hover before the refrigerator shelves, "Elvira!"
As I sit and stare upon blankness, "Elvira!"

Again, invincibly, like a geographical fact,
Or the necessary difference in a memory,
Or the inevitable, insistent fate of every living thing,
She has yelled the name "Elvira!"
The vessels of sense are brimming with Elviras
And I want to fix the name Elvira
In a matrimony with its fact
And bring these arbitrary resonances to a beginning.
So, Elvira, I now recognize all shapes

That can be figured from your name:
Earl of the real in my vale or lair,
Alive with ire, I'll rail in the vile air's ear,
I'll rile my liver with evil ale, and call
All invisible births to fall
Into a gentle place. Child, your dinner
Waits with its silent commentary of silverware.
Come home, sit, eat, and make things peaceful again.
Smooth out and soothe the day's slow passage
With your singular and blessed girlhood.

Shimmering with hazy exhaustion,
Half dead, lumbering over itself, immense,
The afternoon becomes another piece of history,
And ponders the long, rich slide into evening.
Then, with equivalent stress on each syllable,
As if to test the tenuous connection of her tongue
To every bit of the beyond, going higher
Than any one name could ever hope to aspire,
"Gina!" yells my muse, "Gina!"

ASTORIA BOULEVARD

— for D. J.

On Astoria Boulevard, in Queens, strolling
The tilted pavement past birdsong and crack,
I note that plastic stuck in trees turns black.
An illustrated train clanks by, rolling

Through the thick March fog that calls forth filth and squalor
From old snowbanks. A soggy mattress lies
Half off the curb, like a drunk. A squad car flies
Past as I lean on the door of a pizza parlor,

John's Old Time Pizzeria, a Greek place.
I order a meatball hero and a beer,
Then slouch at a table. Why does she live here?
I ask myself again, rubbing my face.

Indifferently surrendering buildings squat
Like every bad choice you ever made. There are
No lawns worth a dog, prosperity sleeps far
Across the water, in ice-pick spires. Lives clot

And go on staring out of windows or
Pull tangled laundry from machines as the cars
Shuttle from homes to stores to jobs to bars.
I was still chewing on this curse when the door

Flopped open like a pigeon's dirty wing
When it's had enough of being teased and followed
By a child who must be shown what can be hollowed
Out of the air, just how the funny thing

Could always fly. Two boys fell on the floor,
One yelling "Leggo!" the other holding on,
Announcing "No first down, folks." Two more, pawns
Cracking my thoughtful grid, rolled through the door

And crashed on the linoleum. In the kitchen
A guy with bad beard holding a pot lid
Looked out, shook his head, turned back to sniff. One kid
Got up, brushed off his bluejeans, and said "Bitchin'."

Then like a wave of summer tar-heat, they
Rose to the counter and hung there, eyeing my beer.
Fats yelled "I'm 21! I want a beer!"
"Yeah, give us beers," the others shouted, "Hey!

How about a little attention here? A Bud!"
The man working the counter leaned on the wall
And said "Wait a couple years. Then you have all
You want." Cold drafts again. The door went thud

And a woman said "John, you shouldn't tell them that."
John said "Helena," and picked his teeth. The boys,
Now filling a booth, made innovative noise
With silverware. Two got up and ran at

Each other. Right in the middle of the room
They jumped, slapped palms together overhead,
Collided, and fell down. "OK," John said,
"Don't you care I got a customer?" "I threw him

Out of the house," Helena sighed as she sat
On a counter stool, "he's gone." "Wow," said John
And gave her my beer. She looked at it. "Bon
Jovi!" yelled Bitchin', "Shot to the heart! I got

Tickets!" stood up and tossed his fork in the air.
Helena fiddled in her bag to show
She would not cry now, dug up old matches. "Come go
Get your aunt some cigarettes," John called, "over there."

Budweiser took John's quarters to the slot.
A man in white, steam streaming around his head,
Came towards me. "Hot meatball, peppas?" he said.
I nodded and the dish clanked down. "It's hot,"

He warned, then stood there, waiting. I took a bite.
I burned my mouth. A slice of pepper slow-
Ly, juicily, plopped on the plate. "I'm Larry, he's Mo,
You're Curly." "John, where the napkins? Good?" "Just right,"

I slobbered. "Yes. It's good. It hits the spot."

THE SEPTIC TANK

— for the Mallet family, at Varengeville-sur-Mer

1.

I am a young man standing in a cesspool.

At a jointed point triangular with the houses,
Two old clay pipes are spitting filth
From their broken elbow into the dirt.
Thousands of flies fight in the thick, warm air.
Saturated clay where only lean grass grows
Sticks to my boots.

I start to dig again.
Two rusted bolts clamp the curved metal blade
To the spade shaft, which is just long enough,
And bulbs slightly at the free end
So the hand can grip it better.
The blade's edges, sharpened and resharpened,
Are wearing away like a wave.
Use has rubbed the shaft grain smooth.

I've used this spade to cut bed borders,
And regain rows from the rat grass
Smothering the kitchen garden now a nursery.
That sectioned, brittle, endless weed
Grows by extending and knotting itself
Until underground a new shoot buds,
Sprouts ganglia and begins to strangle
Whatever other root it touches.
It digs itself, like foolish habits,
Into boot packed paths. The only way to stop it
Is to turn the dirt six inches deep
And sift it, grasping plants whole,
Wearing gloves that take on filth
Until they lie, when dry, like the empty hands
We give up for work.

2.

The other gardeners come by at noon
To tell me I can knock off for lunch
And to see what I've accomplished.
They have to look down.
I stand next to the jutting pipes.
Earthenware chips are scattered around my feet
In a slippery sloppy hole a meter deep.
What are you doing down there, they say,
Digging to China? My dear Baron,
Do you know there's shit in your hair?
They laugh. Someone knocks out a Gitane for me.

I have begun to speak the patois of sex,
Food, drink, sleep, excrement, work, and death —
Who's going to kill that mole this afternoon,
The busy one near the hydrangeas? I will, I say.
I'll wait with a spade and bash his brains in,
The way you said, third time he surfaces,
Pushing the final load of dirt
Up out of his lawn ripping hole.

I take the cigarette and smoke it.
Sweat is running into my eyes again.
The head gardener reaches down to me.
Cigarette in my lips, right glove and spade shaft
In my left, gloved hand, I take hold of his right hand
With my right, brace my left foot
Against the wall of the little pit,
And climb out.

3.

In a garden there's a right
Way and a wrong way to do everything. It's different
From the nettle groves, pastures, unbridled night
Of thickets and woods outside, where whatever works

Is good. For example, we keep the grass at the height
We want, an even, regular crop,
Good for walking and lying on in the green light.
There are places where the power mowers

Cannot turn, wet, marshy corners tight
With mosses and roots and stones. We let them go.
But they lie mostly out of sight,
Hidden away from the formal patterns,

Dank pools below the paths where Chinese lilies
Clutch the mud, only flowerheads visible in the bright
Gaze of the paying visitor who walks on gravel
That we have raked. We craft delight from knowing

What judgments make the polite patterns
Of any garden's dirty discourse work —
Grubs, aphids, moles, the parasite killing the elms,
And other self-slaughters carefully cut back, shoveled away,

Dissolved, and spread into humus at each site
Where they can do some good by dying.
We work by day. And in a form of pay
The day works all night, every night,

Growing into each plant, however slight.